Stone by Design

Stone by Design

THE ARTISTRY OF LEW FRENCH

Photographs by Alison Shaw

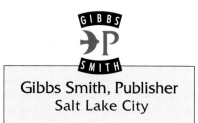

Gibbs Smith, Publisher
Salt Lake City

First Edition

09 08   8 7

Published by

Gibbs Smith, Publisher

P.O. Box 667

Layton, Utah 84041

Orders: 1.800.748.5439

www.gibbs-smith.com

Designed by Steve Rachwal

Printed and bound in Hong Kong

Library of Congress Cataloging-in-Publication Data

French, Lew.

Stone by design : the artistry of Lew French / photographs by Alison Shaw.—1st ed.

  p. cm.

ISBN 10:1-58685-443-7   ISBN 13:978-1-58685-443-0

1. French, Lew—Homes and haunts. 2. Stonemasons—United States.

3. Building, Stone—United States. 4. Decoration and ornament, Architectural. 5.

Stonemasonry—Pictorial works. I. Shaw, Alison, 1953- II. Title.

TH140.F74A3 2005

721'.0441—dc22

2005010337

Lew French can be contacted by mail at P.O. Box 1122 Vineyard Haven, MA 02568, or by email at lew_french_stone@yahoo.com.

This book is dedicated to my mother, Doris French,

and to the memory of my father, Bill.

Mom, thank you for your help and support throughout my life.

"There are sermons in stone and books in rivulets."

—KIRPAL SINGH

CONTENTS

PREFACE

Checking my answering machine after coming home from work one day, I found a message from Madge Baird, editor for Gibbs Smith, Publisher. Madge was contacting me after having seen a feature article on my stonework in the August 2000 issue of *House Beautiful* magazine. She asked me if I would be interested in having a coffee-table book of my stonework published. After our conversation, I thought seriously about the proposal. Finally, four years later, I have decided to do it. The problem I face is that I am basically a private person. By publishing my lifework, I am definitely revealing myself to a broader public than Martha's Vineyard. The island is where most of my work is. Here is where I feel comfortable with who I am and what I do. Showing so much of my work in one book through Alison Shaw's images is exposing enough, but also being asked by Madge to write about the work — explain to strangers with words what these stone pieces, the things that I build, mean to me — I find even more daunting.

However, although the physical work manifested in these pictures is the purpose of this book, I realize that it is quite a different thing to see these tactile pieces of stonework in person than to see them in a photo, no matter how fine the photograph. It is this realization that has encouraged me to tell the stories and process behind these pieces.

Ironically, while I sit here putting pen to paper to say "This is what I think," the most difficult aspect of what I do is to try not to think. Clearing my mind is a challenge, but I have found that this is when my best works and ideas transpire — when my mind is calm and clear.

As you read through this book, I hope you will sense not only the power stone has, but also the personal way it becomes part of a landscape or a home and then people's lives.

A blanket of fresh snow covers the winter landscape of a walled garden.

ACKNOWLEDGMENTS

First, I would like to thank my family for their patience and support during the process of making this book: Asa and Truman, how fortunate I am to have you both for sons; my sister, Lisa, her husband, Scott, and their children, Carrie and Bill.

A special thanks to Claudia Macedo for her input, encouragement, and understanding, not only throughout the development of this book, but also during the past four years of our relationship.

I am deeply grateful to my mom, Doris, who helped me with the spelling and rewriting of my original manuscript, transforming it into a more legible piece of work.

My deepest appreciation goes to John and Judi for helping Claudia, Truman, Asa, and me in so many ways. Claudia and I are indebted to both of you. From my family to yours, thank you for being more than our friends.

I am especially grateful to all my friends who have helped me throughout my working career. Richard, Steven, Renee, Tom and Lucia Iammarino; Bart and Julie Thorpe; Fran and David Flanders; Ronaldo Oligario da Silva; Patrick and Colin Carr; Jay Walsh; Phyllis McMorrow for her garden expertise; and George Arsenault, my stone supplier and friend, who throughout our relationship has treated me fairly and honestly, always trying to accommodate my stone needs to the best of his abilities.

I would like to extend a special thanks to all my clients who have given me the opportunity to work with them over the last twenty-five years, enabling me to design and create my stonework. Thank you for your trust and the freedom to explore what can be done with stone.

To all the architects and designers I have been fortunate enough to be associated with, especially Bruce MacNelly, Linda Cohen, Joseph Dick, Ivan Bereznicki, and Randy Correll from the architectural firm of Robert A. M. Stern, thank you.

Madge Baird and the people at Gibbs Smith, Publisher, thank you. A special note of gratitude to Johanna Buchert Smith, my editor, for listening to and understanding

A natural break or cleft in a weathered, lichened piece of fieldstone.

my points of view and working so hard to produce the best book possible. I will always remember your interest and kindness towards me.

For the help that Mom received from our Zumbrota connections, Phyllis Groth and Becky Gill.

Thanks to Oscar Hansen, my island connection, for all his help typing and preparing the rough manuscript for the publisher. Thanks to Claire Cain and Sue Dawson for all their efforts in Alison's studio.

Finally, I am especially thankful to Alison Shaw for all her hard work and creative input. She spent untold hours in all kinds of weather conditions to try to get the right camera shots. Her dedication to her art form is apparent in all her work. Alison has brought so much of her incredible talent and energy to this book; I have really enjoyed working with her. Truly, I am lucky that she chose to photograph my work. Thank you, Alison, for your commitment to our book.

INTRODUCTION

WORKING WITH STONE FOR THE PAST TWENTY-EIGHT YEARS HAS BEEN ONE CONTINUOUS LEARNING EXPERIENCE FOR ME. I HAVE DESIGNED AND BUILT A WIDE VARIETY OF STONE OBJECTS, INCLUDING FIREPLACES, WALLS, GARDENS, PATIOS, INTERIOR SPACES, SCULPTURES, AND LAND-SCAPES. THROUGHOUT ALL THIS CREATING AND BUILDING, I AM STILL AMAZED AT HOW MUCH I DO NOT KNOW OR UNDERSTAND ABOUT THIS SIMPLE AND BASIC MATERIAL CALLED STONE.

An ancient fissured stone is mounted to a driftwood base, making a small desktop sculpture.

I had just turned nineteen when I first used stone in a building project. I sensed that there was something special about stone, but I did not begin to realize its full potential until I built a black limestone exterior chimney about three years later. While working on the chimney, the full force of the stone's power and energy hit me. It was an awakening. I remember to this day going to the quarry, handpicking the stones to be used, mixing the cement powder with the washed sand to make the concrete to hold the stones in place. I was doing all the work myself, putting in twelve-hour days of backbreaking labor. At night I would find myself in bed, exhausted from the day's work in the hot sun but still unable to fall asleep, just lying there on my back. I waited anxiously for daybreak so I could go back to work and lay more stone, thoughts racing through my mind, excited about the hypnotic energy that the emerging patterns of the stones were creating. I wanted to create a bigger picture, to set my tools down at the end of the day and just stare at what was unfolding. It was not about the work—I liked being outdoors, working for myself, and being physically active. But the physical work was just a means to the end: the completed six-by-twenty-two-foot rectangular form. When it was finished, I could not stop myself from looking at it. The visual impact the stonework had on me was like nothing I had experienced in my young life. For the first time I knew what I wanted to do: I wanted to work with stone.

I don't remember the name of the owner of the house. I do remember he lived about twenty miles north of St. Paul, Minnesota. He was a businessman of some sort. I talked to him very little and didn't have the opportunity to get to know him. When the job was complete, I felt strange to have been affected by stone in such an odd way. It is difficult to share with anyone the impact that experience had on me—how do you try to make someone else understand what is happening to you when you cannot comprehend what is going on yourself?

After the chimney was completed, I returned to my client's house on only two different occasions. Surprisingly, both times, when I turned the corner and approached the stonework, there stood the owner staring at the stones.

The first time, going back to gather my tools and equipment, I exchanged greetings with him. We said very little between us. I collected my construction things, loaded my truck and left. The second time I went to pick up my final check. Instead of going to the front door and announcing myself, I went to see the chimney first. There stood the owner of the house, almost in the same spot, intently looking at the stonework. I could tell that he felt a little uncomfortable or maybe awkward, as if I had caught him in a situation he could not explain. I walked over, stood beside him and looked. For about a minute, we stood in silence, absorbed in the image of the stone. He finally broke the silence by saying, "You know, it is the strangest thing; there's something about these stones that draws me here, that makes me want to look at them."

I realized with a certain sense of relief that I was not alone with my feelings the stonework images were creating inside me. He had also been awakened by the power of stone.

The presence that stone has is not just what we see but how we feel in and around it. When I think about it, stones of every size, shape, and variety can be found almost anywhere on earth. Even if they are not exposed on the ground, they are probably just underneath our feet. The visual impact stone has on our senses is as powerful as most media used in art. Not only are the magnificent historical buildings constructed of stone, but they also housed individual stones sculpted into masterpieces by artists who could coax their own ideas and inner visions from blocks of granite and marble.

ABOVE: *The locust tree rafter has been centered on the arched window's highest point. The tail of the wooden rafter has been left untrimmed.*

RIGHT: *The force created by driving iron wedges into the stone's predrilled holes has split the stone mass in half.*

LEFT: *A keystone locks into place the thinner, slightly wedge-shaped stones that make an arch.*

BELOW: *A present for one of my clients, this wall hanging is made of five stones and driftwood. The frame was created from old chestnut barn board.*

Natural uncut stone has been used in many different ways by almost all cultures. Stone has been used for basic utilitarian needs: rough shelters, walls for defense or safety purposes, pens for livestock, even the roads that Roman legions traveled on. In the Japanese heritage, stoneworkers integrated stone into people's lives, creating gardens that give a deep sense of calm, serenity, and harmony. Throughout the centuries, the Japanese have become masters of stone placement in relation to the elements of the surrounding landscapes—hills, mountains, valleys and plateaus, water, light, trees, shrubs, bamboos, flowers, grasses, and many different varieties of moss. Man-made structures, including houses and buildings, are also incorporated. All of these components combine with stone to make exquisite gardens and peaceful living spaces.

Stone left in its natural shape has a power and drama that is not only seen but also felt. An example of this is conveyed in the stone ruins of pre-Christian cultures on the British Isles. We can only speculate on the meanings behind the thousands of stone circles, standing stones, cairns, dolmens, and groupings that are left for us to experience. Energy seems to be emitted not only from the stones themselves but also from their relationships to one another and the landscape around them.

This, I believe, is the lasting legacy of stone—a universal bond from past to present. From the Japanese gardens at the Kyoto Imperial Palace to the mystery of Stonehenge, there is a commonality of elements that either enhances the essence of the stonework or detracts from the overall effect of it.

For me, identifying and understanding the elements that make some designs more pleasing than others has been a lifelong process. When broken down, some of the components are size, shape, color, texture, harmony, rhythm, balance, tension, and scale. Within this framework, patterns emerge. When used well these elements and the stones themselves take on a life of their own.

The techniques for fitting stones to other stones have varied throughout history. Cutting square or rectangular shapes out of larger formations of stones or quarries and then fitting the sides together was a common approach shared by the Egyptian pyramid builders, European cathedral makers, and South and Central American Mayans, Incas, and Aztecs. Throughout most periods in history, civilizations around the world have employed this type of building technique. For myself, I can only wonder and marvel at how these varied cultures built their edifices and monuments without the help of cranes, backhoes, and excavators. These builders had no power tools to split and shape the stone, and no cement trucks mixing and pouring concrete to lay the foundations for stone structures to rest. Roman engineers used vast quantities of concrete in their private and public works, but the secret of making concrete was lost with the fall of Rome and only rediscovered in the 1800s. Roman concrete is studied to this very day for its strength and durability.

Ancient stoneworkers could not utilize all of the conveniences that I take for granted in this modern world. I always try not to alter the visible face of the stones, but when I need to reshape a part of a stone where its fresh-cut edge will not be seen, I just fire up my diamond-tipped-bladed gas-engine cutoff saw. In minutes, after creating clouds of dust, I have accomplished what could have taken days or weeks for a crew of Greek temple builders in 400 BC to do. One thing that hasn't changed though: after lifting and moving stone all day I can certainly sympathize with those ancient stoneworkers' fatigue.

Growing up in a small town surrounded by farms in southern Minnesota, I was introduced to the basics of building with masonry—concrete, cement block, and brick—by my father's friend Leonard Lundgren. He was my teacher. Not only was Len a pleasant person, he was also an old-school craftsman versed in all aspects of construction, who valued and took pride in what he knew and how he did his work. Len showed me, through example, how to develop concepts and ideas not only before starting the work, but also during the building process itself. He taught me to have a concept, yet remain open to what was unfolding, and then to follow in the direction that the piece was leading me. Though we did very few stone projects together, he gave me the beginnings I needed to develop and see numerous ways of working with stone.

I try to observe stone in nature. By placing myself in the stone's environment, I try to understand what I sense, but more importantly, what I see. I try to quiet my mind and let as many natural impressions as possible enter. I then interpret the thoughts and formulate ideas for my designs.

My preferred technique in laying stone is to not alter the shape or redefine it. I try to leave it in its found, or natural, state, letting the shape of the stone speak for itself. My job is to see the character and strengths of the stone's shape and how it relates to the next stone in a cohesive and harmonious manner. I do, in certain designs, like to combine totally unaltered stones with particular accent stones that have been reshaped by the stoneworkers that came before me.

Most of my work is what is called the dry-stack look. Traditionally on Martha's Vineyard and throughout New England, the classic walls that mark the fields and boundaries have no cement or mortar in the joints to hold them together. It is one stone bearing directly on another stone that creates the tension that supports the pieces holding them in place. With a dry-stack wall, gravity is the overriding rule that must be followed. The test for placing a stone in the dry-stack format is simple:

Blocks of granite form steps that support the large lintel stone, making a frame for the warming fire.

If the stone looks at rest, it is at rest; however, if a stone is out of sync or precariously balanced, gravity will eventually make it fall.

No matter how successful my visions of stone are, by comparison to the perfection of the works of nature, I realize they are pale imitations of the physical world. It is very difficult to try and physically reproduce what you experience when you open your senses to the natural world. One of the highest compliments that I receive about my work is when someone tells me my work looks like it has always been there. My works, depending on the application, may or may not have cement mortar in them, but I prefer the look of solidity achieved by dry-stacking stone, one stone's shape accepting the other's form. For me, this style first and foremost evokes a visually hypnotic pattern that draws in my senses. Still, after all these years of work it is hard to stop looking at and analyzing the effect produced by stone.

If the nature of the stone and the combining of the stones are highlighted by the stoneworker, the completed piece should gently focus your attention and draw you in visually and emotionally. Accentuating the energy that is latent in stone is the purpose of my work. More than a quarter of a century ago, through nature, I was drawn to the power of stone. With good fortune, being at the right place at the right time, I have been able to design and create my own style of stonework. I continually feel the energy and power that stone generates, but most of all I feel thankful for the opportunity to do my work.

TRANSFORMATIONS IN STONE

A Writing Studio

IT IS AN IRONY THAT PARTS OF THIS BOOK WERE WRITTEN IN A SMALL STONE BUILDING, A WRITING STUDIO I CREATED FIVE YEARS AGO FOR JUDI, ONE OF MY CLIENTS—AN IRONY, I AM SURE, NOT LOST ON HER.

I was informed by a local resident familiar with the history of the original stone building that it was constructed in the 1920s to be used as a spring-house for keeping foods cool in the warmer months. Judi wanted an intimate space away from the main house to be able to work on her writing without interruptions—mainly, she says tongue in cheek, her husband and three children.

The lack of light was the room's most critical design problem. The building was of historical importance, so it could not be altered to have electricity; that was part of an agreement with the town's building committee. Two main problems stood in the way of converting the stone structure into a pleasant, usable area: one, the building's small size, and two, its dark and dank interior space.

To address the second problem, a new roof with a skylight had just been completed, though the original dirt floor remained. Redoing the floor seemed like the logical place to start. Pouring a subfloor of concrete not only made a stable base to start the stone floor on, it also provided a barrier from the damp ground. My helper and I started gathering fieldstone from my surplus stone pile, choosing each stone for its small size and flatness. We then individually ground what would be the stone's exposed face with

Interior of writing studio. A combination of stones, driftwood, and layers of stucco on the walls makes it a pleasant place to write in.

ABOVE: *Filling a depression on the wall created a mosaic of stone and driftwood.*

LEFT: *A mixture of fieldstones and fir wood make up the floor of the writing studio.*

RIGHT: *Driftwood shelves placed on the ledges of the original stone wall are held in place by the portland-based cement stucco.*

a diamond-tipped grinding machine, not because the surface needed to be flatter still, though it would make walking easier, but because the ground face of a stone is much lighter in color and this would help illuminate the room. The small mosaic scale of the stone combined with the rock's newfound light color went a long way in making the room appear and feel larger than it is. Resolving the floor was one step closer to resolving the building's problems of size and light.

Next was the question of the remaining interior of the building. The stone walls in the inside of the building had a rough, broken texture, and had been made out of large split stones. The proportion of the large stone in such a small area, and the darker tones of their uneven surfaces, made the space feel claustrophobic and oppressive. Locating the room's major focal points, I built small sections of stone walls and inlays into the existing pockets or depressions around and in between the big rocks.

The uneven thickness of the split stones had created these ledged niches when the original walls were built. In other strategic areas, I covered them by using varying shapes, sizes, and patterns of gray-to-brown driftwood. Using a white portland-based cement with native sand, we stuccoed the remaining wall surfaces. By building up the walls' surfaces with three coats of stucco, it gave the now-somewhat-flattened walls a tone of depth that made the room more appealing and warm.

The creamy white plaster-like stucco that surrounds the driftwood and stone highlights their colors and textures. The stucco also gives a solid backdrop for the lines created from fitting the individual pieces together. By bringing the exposed stone to scale with the size of the building and using lighter colors inside, the overall effect of the finished room was one of space, harmony, and light.

Judi's only complaint is that now the writing studio is such a pleasant place to be, everyone, including her family, shows up and disturbs her writing. The little stone studio has turned out to be a magnet for her family and friends, a special gathering place during the long summer months.

The studio sits in a mowed field with an incredibly beautiful and expansive water view over a flowering wild meadow that descends right to the ocean's edge. During the period of working on the writing studio, I could not help but think of what a great spot this field would be to make a stone patio with a circular fire pit. I could imagine sitting around the blazing bonfire on the Vineyard's cool, clear, starry summer nights, listening to the waves break on the beach and smelling the fragrance that only the sea produces.

ABOVE: Designing a Gothic-style arch creates a niche in the standing wall.

RIGHT: The natural, raised shape in the large granite piece made me want to repeat the form in small fieldstones.

LEFT: *Bonfire on a cool, gray day.*

BELOW: *The three bench stones mark the eight-foot-diameter fire pit.*

RIGHT: *The first glimpse of sunlight on the wall after the snow clouds disappear.*

*"Behind the privacy of the high stone wall,
it's just you, the meadow, and the ocean."*

One other distinct concept that kept going through my head in conjunction with the fire pit was to create a high wall of stone to provide a privacy screen from the view of the main house and guesthouse. Once behind the standing stone wall, you would be totally secluded from the activities of the surrounding property: just you, the meadow, and the ocean.

The following summer, after one year of the studio's use, I proposed my thoughts and ideas for enhancing the exterior space around her writing retreat. Judi seemed genuinely excited about the concept of a fire pit and an L-shaped, freestanding wall. She told me that she and her husband would discuss the project. When I next saw her, I of course asked her what they decided. She laughed and said, "We want you to go ahead and do it," adding that they had decided it would be her birthday present. To have the opportunity to create such a powerful and beautiful piece of work would be, in a way, a birthday present for me also; it would be a gift for the both of us.

ABOVE: *The short side of the L-shaped wall is bathed in a warm golden glow during the height of the island's summer.*

LEFT: *Independent standing stones border the outside edge of the patio surrounding the fire pit.*

ABOVE: A grass pathway runs between the raised patios behind the standing stones.

LEFT: Combining large vertical granite stones and small fieldstones made a private screen from the guest house and main house.

BELOW: The standing stone wall just before dark.

ABOVE: *The stone portal is one of the three main visual anchor points to the design of the fire pit area, the other two being the standing wall and writing studio.*

RIGHT: *Flowers and shrubs always add a soft touch to stone.*

"I could imagine sitting around the blazing bonfire on the Vineyard's cool, clear, starry summer nights listening to the waves break on the beach."

LANDSCAPING WITH STONE

The Quitsa Pond Project

WHEN I FIRST MET MY FUTURE CLIENTS, THE THREE OF US WERE GUESTS AT A SUMMER PARTY THAT WAS BEING HELD ON A GRAND-SCALED, WEATHERED GRANITE PATIO THAT I HAD RECENTLY COMPLETED. LITTLE DID I KNOW THAT I WOULD SPEND APPROXIMATELY FIVE YEARS OF MY LIFE DESIGNING, BUILDING, AND LANDSCAPING THE GARDENS AROUND THEIR BEAUTIFUL HOUSE AND BUILDING SITE.

On one side of the lot is a tidal salt marsh filled with native plants, birds, and wildlife. The site also borders Quitsa Pond, the middle pond in a trio that all connect to the ocean at the small fishing village of Menemsha. It is a stunning setting to create and work in.

I spent the first two years designing and physically doing the work in the different stone aspects of the job—the stone foundations for the buildings, the grade-retaining walls and freestanding boundary walls, the stone patios, landings, sidewalks, and the sculptural stones in the garden spaces. The stonework in my designs is the framing element, so it becomes the dominant feature of the hardscaping, which eventually becomes the bones, or skeleton, of the entire landscape. In my terms, hardscape means the totalness of the landscape, so anything that is not a plant is hardscape. The key to a flowing, harmonious design is to complement the other established hardscape features such as hills, valleys, flat spaces, water and, of course, the man-made element of the buildings themselves. As a landscape

The only stone on the property prior to the landscaping was this huge glacial erratic, too heavy to be moved. The sidewalk through the grounds was built around it.

designer, I may choose to create separate areas of interest, but I must maintain unifying threads of material, concept, and direction ending in a cohesive whole that enhances the undisturbed natural setting of sky, land, and water.

The work unfolded in stages. One aspect of the project led to the next, starting with the stone foundation of the boathouse, set about ten feet back from the water's edge. The boathouse design by architect Joseph Dick is simple but stylized. I felt that the stone foundation should respect his intent of design and complement his vision. Instead of choosing old-wall fieldstone that was just round and uniform in shape, I selected stones that had more dramatic faces and variety in their profiles, thus creating a more evolved style and intriguing look.

In the next phase I defined the property with a double-face, dry-stack stone wall. The wall itself is three feet high and more than one thousand feet long. Its inspiration was an existing wall built by farmers in the late 1700s, whose start was lost over the ridge of the horizon, but whose tumbledown end was definitely in the salt marsh by the boathouse.

As the new wall was being built, the general contractor constructed the large main house. Like the boathouse, the main house also rests on a stone foundation. Poured-concrete walls hold the house structure, which made my job easier. With the stone acting as a twelve-inch veneer, I don't have to worry about the foundation's structural integrity. Allowing at least twelve inches of space between the face of the stone and the start of the concrete wall gave me plenty of room to do my stonework. Most of the house needed to be complete before I could start the landscaping process, because the elevation of the house is the determining point for the landscape grades. Trying to integrate the sprawling building into its natural surroundings was the challenge. I decided the solution to the problems posed by the multiple grade changes would be to use retaining walls in addition to stone boulders, sculptural groupings of stones, and large flat pieces of granite to make patios. These different choices of elements within the hardscape started to become more apparent as I worked on the site. By creating a plan that incorporated all different kinds of stonework, I resolved the problems of grade changes.

On the hillside bordering the tidal salt marsh, I used large boulders that had been exposed to the New England climate for years. Rocks the size of a kitchen stove had developed the weather-aged patina that gives stone an ancient, grounded feel, and colonies of lichen and mosses covered their surfaces. It is choosing the right stones that makes a new piece of work seem old. Using these large glacial erratics in unison with small weathered fieldstones, I built a set of retaining walls that starts from the house's stone foundation and ends at the point where it meets the hillside's grade.

The Quitsa Pond project began with the creation of the boathouse's stone foundation.

The stones used around this window are angled to allow a wide field of vision when looking out from the interior.

With the larger stones protruding out from the face of the smaller stones in the retaining wall, it highlighted the sculptural beauty of each of the base anchor stones. The texture of the wall becomes more intriguing and interesting in a curving, sweeping profile. The form of the wall mimics the rhythm created by the vegetation at the edge of the marsh: a line of long-stemmed grasses produces a gentle, sweeping, back-and-forth motion, guiding the eye along the face of the wall and creating a sense of movement. The visual impact of these walls is due to their contrast in size, texture, and overall shape.

At the completion of the stone stages of the project, I had purchased and trucked down from the woods of Maine more than 200 tons of weathered boulders of field-stone, flat gray and pink granite for patios, and mixed sizes of old wall stone for stepping stones, foundation veneers, and walls. Ironically, the only large stone origi-nally on the property that could be incorporated into the design plan was so big that it could not be moved by a tractor backhoe. At the ground's surface, it was about the size of two wheelbarrows and protruding from the grass line twenty-four inches into the air. The boulder appeared to be relatively large, but something that should easily be moved with the machine. What we could see turned out to be only the tip of the iceberg. Trying to relocate the stone proved to be impossible. With the bulk of the mass buried in the ground, the stone's permanent resting place was about thirty feet from the house's main entrance.

In the random-pattern fieldstone patio I was just completing, I left certain areas strategically free of stones, choosing to fill the voids with plants. Some plants I favor with stone are red, white, and purple wooly thymes; different varieties of the mint family; low, creeping sedums; potentillas; and Irish mosses. Of all the plants I use, the different types of thymes are my favorite. The majority of the plants I use to plant with stone patios are generally low growers that can withstand foot traffic. Mixing the right balance of green living material provides softness that contrasts with the hard quality of the stone.

Capping the larger planted entrance patio is an elevated landing, which is the final approach to the main entrance door. My design idea was to connect the front entrance patio to the parking area with a stone sidewalk. The problem was, the direc-tion of the path led directly into the native large boulder.

Over the years I have found that a perceived problem can often turn out to be a blessing in disguise. Setbacks or problems make you work harder at developing alter-nate concepts so you have more choices to use in the overall design. My plan was not going to work, and it would be necessary for me to adjust what I wanted to do. So instead of moving the rock, I simply encircled it with the sidewalk stones,

"I have learned to trust my instincts when it comes to design. If it feels right, I go with it."

keeping the edge of the walkway roughly twelve inches back from the boulder, creating a planting bed between the two stone surfaces. The problem of what to do with the stone sticking out of the ground like a sore thumb actually became a really interesting design feature. The boulder's weathered, lichened, vertical presence added a grounded focal point to the flat plane of the sidewalks.

Working on-site at the beginning of the project and representing the client's interest was a man named Bart Thorpe. Bart is basically a jack-of-all-trades, and he was there to facilitate the progress of the job. I liked Bart right away. To me, at that point in our relationship, Bart's best quality was that he owned a backhoe tractor and he knew how to use it. It was a promising start for a beautiful friendship, because I was a stonemason with hundreds of tons of stone to move and set. For the following two years Bart and I worked together almost daily, lifting, moving, and setting stones for the retaining and freestanding walls. We backfilled hillsides with the site's sandy soil, giving the retaining walls their purpose and meaning. We created the hills and valleys that turned out to be the skin of the finished grades, spreading the humus-rich loam that would provide the nutrients for the grass, lawns, and flowers to come. All of this was done by Bart with his machine and me with my smaller skid loader, or Bobcat.

Bart turned out to be an excellent backhoe operator. Patience and caution are two attributes that are critical in someone controlling a machine that is lifting and placing a dangling stone on a chain that may weigh up to three and a half tons, pushing the machine to its working limits. The nature of doing stonework puts you at physical risk. One slip, one jerky movement with the arm of the backhoe, one mistake and someone could end up in the hospital or worse. When working with stone I prefer to have the workspace as quiet as possible. The fewer distractions, the more I can concentrate on the work at hand and the safer I feel. Building with stone has its inherent dangers. By creating a noisy, chaotic environment, you multiply your chances of becoming injured. While working with Bart on the Quitsa Pond job, and since then on numerous other projects, I've developed a trust and respect not only for his abilities with his machine, but also for his no-nonsense opinions and judgments when it comes to the building of the projected designs.

Finally, after two years' worth of trips to New Hampshire and Maine to gather stone, with Bart's input and help, the overall stonework and hardscaping were complete. I had not realized when I had started the stone foundation for the boathouse two years earlier that this would turn out to be such a major project. The scale and intensity had pretty much drained me both physically and emotionally, and I was looking for a short break from work. I was more than a little surprised when my clients then asked me to do the softscape, the garden plantings.

PAGES 40–41: Two chairs, ten feet from the inn's stone suite, invite viewers to watch the activities around the pond. Ducks, geese, ospreys, red-tailed hawks, muskrats, deer, raccoons, rabbits, turtles, and horses, all at different times of the day, congregate at the water's edge.

LEFT: A wintery view of Bliss Pond, just behind the oak trees. Usually the Vineyard has mild winters, but during the colder stretches it's possible to ice skate or play hockey on the pond.

"What do I know about gardening?" I asked, adding, "I'm just a stonemason." My client answered, "You did the flowers at Bliss Pond Farm, right?" To drive home my point of being a stonemason, I spoke as one, in the short, pointed way that comes from working all day with inanimate objects: "Yeah, I guess." He said, "That's what we want, lots of flowers. Do what you did over there." We discussed the hopes and expectations for the plantings, and the dialogue ended as he turned and walked back to his house.

Bliss Pond Farm is another name for the Captain Flanders Inn, an up-island bed-and-breakfast on the Menemsha Crossroads, less than one mile from the town of Chilmark. My friends Bart and Julie Thorpe are the proprietors of the inn.

The original building, constructed in the 1740s, was still in good condition. I had proposed the idea of re-landscaping the surroundings and main entrance to the house. A worn-out grassy lawn led from the parking area to the front door. I felt a warmer and more welcoming approach could be created with stone and flowering plants. Some parts of the new landscape would consist of native fieldstone walls, stone entry steps, an arbor and trellis of locust trees, and a stone patio. One of the major components of redesigning the landscape would be choosing and planting the flowering annuals, perennials, and shrubs that would fill the newly created planting beds. This would be the second time that I had also done the plantings in conjunction with my stonework.

Bart has turned out to be one of my closest friends. Sometimes he seems more of a sarcastic brother than a friend. To this day I think he let me plant the gardens, not because, as my ego-driven mind wants to believe, he saw some hidden potential in me for garden design, but because he somehow knew he would not have to pay me for doing it. In the finest New England Yankee tradition the most he would have to do to square the deal would be to barter for my labor with some choice fieldstones from his family's craggy and rocky farm fields in Chilmark that I coveted for their sculptural qualities—in everyone's mind, a fair bargain for all.

Spring on Martha's Vineyard can be very unpredictable. The surrounding waters of the ocean keep the island cooler than the mainland. So even in late May and mid-June it can still be raw and cold. Then, the very next day or two, summer settles in for its welcome season. It was a warm sunny day in late May as I was planting the final batch of one of my favorite flowering annuals, Sky Rocket snapdragons, in a large bed that borders the inn's guest parking area, when I started to think of my childhood summers in my grandmothers' gardens. Little did I know as a child how much I would appreciate and enjoy working with plants as an adult.

The rounded, warm-toned
stones used for the inn's suite
were collected from pastures
and fields on the surrounding farmland.

ABOVE: *A segment of fieldstone wall built over a large boulder outcropping.*

LEFT: *A section of one of the many Quitsa Pond project walls.*

As I was growing up, both of my grandmothers loved working in their large gardens. Grandma Schiller, whose maiden name was Muyres and heritage was German, lived in a small town in northern Minnesota. Grandma French, whose maiden name was Jones and heritage was Welsh, lived in southern Minnesota. Every season they raised fruits and vegetables to eat fresh, canning the surplus to stock the pantry shelves for the long, cold winter. Grandma Schiller was a great baker. I remember gathering apples from her four apple trees so she could bake ten to fifteen pies at a time — some to eat right away, some to freeze for winter. In both of their extensive garden plots, they also grew a variety of annual and perennial flowers.

Like almost all kids in gardening families, my sister, Lisa, and I, hated the idea of working among the garden plants. Against our will, we were forced to work in the dreaded garden. I think the pressure for our "garden experience" came more from our parents, Bill and Doris, than from our kindly old grandmothers.

Now that I have children, I understand that as a parent you are duty-bound to make your kids do things they do not want to do. I am still not quite sure why this is a rule of being a parent. Now, in my middle age, I also have without question sent my two sons, Asa and Truman, out to do their childhood duty battling with our unruly gardens. Shutting out their excuses and verbal protests, I insist they accept their God-given birthright of having "the garden experience." I freely admit some years have been more successful than others. The signs are becoming all too obvious that my sons are growing into men. Summers with their limited work in the garden seem to be over. Now as I tell them to weed or water the garden they just laugh. Asa gets into his green Jeep Cherokee and drives away without a response. Truman, being four years younger and without a driver's license, does not have his brother's options. He goes downstairs to his room, lies on his bed, and starts to read my old copy of Dostoevsky's *The Brothers Karamazov.* I can only assume that one of the statements he is making — the book is very big — is that he's going to be there a long time.

I can muster no verbal response for them and I try not to let them see me smile. After a long hot day of working with stone and plants in my client's gardens, I think to myself, "I don't want to work in our garden either. Let's just buy our veggies in the produce section at the Edgartown Stop & Shop. It's much easier." What kid wants to pull weeds, water plants, pick green beans, and dig potatoes? Does anyone in their right mind think that bending over, chopping with a garden hoe to loosen the soil, sweating in the humid Minnesota summer sun — not to mention being attacked by swarms of deer flies and mosquitoes the size of small birds — is a child's idea of fun?

Fun for Lisa and me was going to the town swimming pool, basking in the sun, doing cannonballs off the low diving board, fishing with Dad on the Zumbro, our local river, or walking five blocks to the only school in town — a combination of elementary, junior high, and senior high — to play games on the playground and to hang out with the more fortunate kids who did not have to work in their family's gardens. Little did I suspect, in my disgruntled twelve-year-old mind, that I actually was learning something practical, and it was something I would grow to love.

After passing each summer's growing season with my grandmothers' gentle guidance, I was becoming aware of the rhythm of nature. The life cycle of the plants slowly started to make sense to me. In the spring you plant the seed, the seed sprouts, the plant grows, the plant flowers, the plant bears fruit, the fruit ripens, the plant slowly starts its steady decline. When the frost comes in the fall, the plant dies. Winter brings the force of the frozen water down from the gray sky to drive the last stubborn seeds from their dead stalks to rest on the hardened earth, lying in wait to be covered by more snow — a blanket protecting them until spring, when the sun's warm rays will create a rebirth in the garden. Without realizing it I was absorbing the beauty of nature. The flowers, plants, insects, earthworms, toads — all the varied living threads combined in an unknowable way to be the fabric of my natural world.

Consciously or not, my grandmothers and parents knew this would be an important part of life's lessons for me. By including me in their world of the garden, like a fully ripened spring seedling planted long ago, I am now the beneficiary of the fruit of their labor.

Many years later, I planted the Quitsa Pond gardens and maintained them for three years, learning more each season on how the different plants I used responded to their seaside environment. Like most gardeners, I chose anchor plants, building and experimenting around them with other plants, trying to complement the established base materials. The gardens proved to be an interesting and large endeavor.

The amount of time spent physically building with stone has a hidden benefit for the design aspect of my work: it forces me mentally to become more aware of my surroundings. It places me in a space to connect with the earth, dig in the island's sandy soil, touch and move the stones, sometimes rolling them end for end, at other times inching them together to see if my intuition of the stone pieces fitting together is correct. Slowly, one by one, the individual shapes accept one another to create the patterns that emerge into the finished whole. When I become part of the slowly unfolding process through the action of the physical labor and the concentration required to do it, ideas and different impressions start to surface in my mind.

Snow covers the double-face wall that starts at the pond's edge and runs the length of the property line.

Architect Joseph Dick and designer Donna Weisman combined their talents to create the main house and boathouse for the Quitsa Pond project.

A partial list of the perennials and annuals I used in the
Quitsa Pond gardens.

PERENNIALS

- Rose coreopsis
- Russian sage
- Moonbeam coreopsis
- Gaillardia
- Nepeta
- Creeping thyme
- Potentilla
- Purple/white coneflower
- Liatris
- Sunflower
- Rudbeckia
- Veronica
- Lavender
- Butterfly bush
- Butterfly weed
- Artemisia
- Rose
- Heather
- Heath
- Salvia
- Flowering oregano
- Yarrow
- Mallow

ANNUALS

- Snapdragon
- Lobelia
- Marigold
- Verbena
- Nicotiana
- Petunia
- Portulaca
- Cleome
- Cosmos
- Ageratum
- Morning glory
- Poppy
- Zinnia

Blocking out random thoughts and trying to stay quiet and focused help me recognize what options are available at the next step of the design.

I try to stay open to the influences of the environment of the space, observing as I build how the stonework is reacting to the surroundings that contain the piece. Adapting the design as I build is always an option if I feel it will help the completed work. In the Quitsa Pond project, it was obvious that the different facets of the job were connected to an outdoor space. The same ideals apply for an interior environment. If I am building a fireplace, I take into account the size and scale of the room, the finished surfaces of the walls, floors and ceilings, and, most important, the likes and dislikes of my clients. The key for discerning their tastes is taking the time to ask the right questions, listening to their answers, and interpreting the information from our discussions. In the end, I have hopefully crafted an individual piece of work that relates and has special meaning to who they are.

When I am working on a concept for a project, in my mind's eye I see the outline of the design. I begin by establishing the main elements, not necessarily each of the details involved. The options of the details present themselves more clearly as the work progresses. It does not matter which materials you are using. Whether it is

Choosing and installing plants was a welcome relief after working two years to build the stone walls, paths, and patios of the Quitsa Pond Project.

The granite patio, with its view to the saltwater pond and marsh, is surrounded by a sculptured landscape of stones and flowering plant beds.

stone, driftwood, wood, cut locust trees, stucco, or plants, whatever the medium, the key to the design is to stay at least one step ahead of the building procedure. At the time, I can instinctively sense if what I am doing seems correct for the design, and I have learned to trust my instincts when I have this feeling. If it feels right, I go with it.

The most challenging aspect of design is to recognize all of the options that are available and how to use them to make a cohesive whole. In the beginning, you have the original idea. Throughout the working process, you need to keep recognizing the maximum amount of choices for the design that might be feasible to do. Then you must decide which direction the work will follow. The end result will be whatever it is. People always ask me at the end of the project if I would have done anything differently. Almost always I say, "No, not really." The work could have turned out different by making other choices and using other options than I had.

What does upset me, though, is when I look back on my work and see a design option that I did not see or recognize. I try to use these instances to learn something about how I am perceiving things and relating my perceptions to a design. Letting my instincts tell me what I am doing at the present is right, responding and going with the direction the work is taking me, not forcing a preconceived idea of what I think should take place but trying to respond to the stone and remain open to what is unfolding. Phase by phase, these are some of the keys to designing my work.

Many years have passed since I set my last fieldstone wall cap in place on the Quitsa Pond project, or planted the final flowering perennial amongst the countless fields of others. When I go back to visit my clients, driving in with the landscape unfolding before me, I am always grateful to them for giving me the opportunity to be able to work and create in such a beautiful environment.

Unable to find a window small enough, I made one of simple leaded glass to fit this space.

"*The boulder's weathered, lichened,
vertical presence added a grounded focal point to
the flat plane of the sidewalks.*"

LEFT: *Leaf debris fallen on a mossy, lichen-covered stone.*

BELOW: A garden path's stepping-stones are spaced apart to allow for plant material to soften and highlight the stone.

Stone retaining walls make possible the grade changes at the main house.

WHEN STONE INSPIRES THE DESIGN

Isabella's Cave

WHEN DAVID FLANDERS KINDLY GAVE ME PERMISSION TO DUMP MY STONE NEXT TO HIS CORNFIELD (OR IS IT A HAY FIELD? FRANKLY, I'VE NEVER NOTICED MUCH OF ANYTHING GROWING THERE), HE HAD NO IDEA HOW QUICKLY STONE, LIKE RABBITS, SEEMS TO MULTIPLY AND GROW ALMOST BY MAGIC.

Mr. Flanders, being a wise Yankee farmer, knows that every year when the spring thaw comes up and out of the ground, it brings with it a fresh crop of stone that was buried under the field's crust. The stone now at the surface has to be gathered and removed before you can plow to prepare your soil for planting seeds. Farmers called this stone "fieldstone." Over the years, these accumulations of stone became the walls that enclosed the fields. Though David knew some other stone-growing phenomenon not tied to the cycle of the seasons was taking place in his farm field, I don't think he knew how much stone I would dump there over the years. "At this rate," he said to himself, "I'll be raising stones, not corn, for my cattle." Action was needed.

Now I find myself threatened monthly by David's son-in-law, Bart. Bart warns me to quit bringing more stone, claiming falsely that I am covering David's field, and remarks, "Geez, David said you could use a part of the field, not the entire fifteen acres." His hollow threat of driving his back-hoe from his house over to the farm and mounding all of my sorted and organized stones into one giant pyramid is wasted on me. I know for a fact

The cool, dark cave looks out to the diving stone, pool, and barn.

ABOVE: *The synchronized curves of this vertical sculpture are completely unaltered; the pieces are not even from the same stone. One was found lying in a pasture field not far from the pool, the other in a pile of stone on a farm more than three miles away.*

LEFT: *Because the pool required a level area and the pasture it is in was sloped, three sides around the pool needed to be retained with stonework. Bella's cave, built into the hillside, is roughly five feet deep and seven feet long. The inside walls are made of fieldstones two feet thick.*

through his wife, Julie, that Bart has too many stone projects at his house for me to help him with to do that. One, of course, is the completion of the stone landscaping around their swimming pool. I have already finished incorporating a stone cave into the design of the retaining wall. The wall structure holds back a seven-foot-high dirt embankment. The inspiration for the cave came when I thought of Bella, their blond, talkative, two-year-old daughter. I was hoping she would enjoy playing inside.

Earlier, while digging back into the high earthen bank, the idea of the cave seemed like a natural extension of the design that was unfolding. While the backhoe's teeth clawed into the soil, I imagined a mysterious cave nestled into the hillside, framed on the top of the ridge by an old five-foot-high combination of fieldstone and cut-stone wall. We found most of the stones used for the cave (and the client's many other projects—a stone diving platform, poolside benches, sculptural accents, stepping stones, and retaining walls) on the farm's eighty acres. Most of the stones were in piles by the field fence lines or in the tumbledown remains of farm walls. On one of the inside corners of the retaining wall, I used some of the split-faced fieldstone left over from the original stone farmhouse of 1858. It was still in a pile in the pasture behind the house.

The post stones and the cave's interior wall stones are set in concrete to make sure the structure is stable. The roof to the cave is made from one piece of stone — a massive six feet by nine feet by eight inches—from a quarry in northern Massachusetts that I had been saving in my collection for fifteen years. It was so heavy that even with his backhoe, Bart struggled to set it on the cave's walls. When Bart and I dug the footings for the irregularly shaped vertical post stones to make the cave opening, we hit extra-fine sugar sand, now the cave's flooring.

Much to my delight, Bella *does* like to go in the cool darkened interior, and she takes her plastic pail and shovel for making sand castles with a little help from her cousins Mariah, Jessica, Oscar, Katie, Erin, and Collin. I always enjoy seeing the things I've built being used, especially by children.

"I found most of the stones in piles by the field fence lines or in tumbledown remains of farm walls."

*With the backdrop of the farm's original fieldstone walls
capped with large split stones, this sculptural stone grouping
sits to the left of the cave's opening.*

ABOVE: *The diving stone is approximately four-and-a-half feet wide and seven feet long and weighs about two and a half tons. Because of the stone's weight, the backhoe had a difficult time setting it on the stone base.*

RIGHT: *The swimming pool is located on what was originally a pasture enclosed by a stone wall.*

ABOVE: *This poolside bench consists of four pieces of dark basalt, one of the oldest and hardest stones on the Vineyard.*

LEFT: *This massive split stone was left over from when the farmhouse was built, in 1858. By combining it with smaller stones, it becomes a visual highlight in this stone retaining wall.*

RIGHT: *One of the cave's two window openings has a view of the Chilmark Community Church.*

*"While the backhoe's teeth clawed into the soil,
        I imagined a mysterious cave nestled into the hillside."*

STONE CRAFTSMANSHIP
Splitting with Feathers and Wedges

THE ISLAND OF MARTHA'S VINEYARD WAS FORMED BY A GLACIER. COMING FROM THE NORTH, THE GLACIER ACTED AS A GIANT, SLOW-MOTION BULL-DOZER AND CONVEYOR BELT, PUSHING AND MOVING ALL DIFFERENT TYPES OF EARTHEN MATERIALS, INCLUDING STONES, WITH IT. AS THE MELTING GLACIER RECEDED NORTH, IT DROPPED ROCKS, SANDS, AND CLAYS INTO THE OCEAN TO FORM THE MASS THAT IS THE ISLAND TODAY.

Stone on the island varies in size from pebble to small house. Interestingly, the island has a wide variety of types and concentrations of stone deposits. In some areas there is no stone at all, just sand and clay. Other places on the island have so many stones that trying to dig a hole with just a shovel is almost impossible—you need a pick or a steel bar to help remove the rock.

Historically, the small stones were removed by hand, and the larger, heavier ones were removed by a team of oxen. The smaller, moveable rocks were used to build dry-stack farm walls, which defined property lines, identified grazing pasture boundaries, and kept livestock in or out, as the case might have been. Farmers would pick the rocks from their fields every spring as the frost left the ground. As the frozen ground thawed, the stones in the soil would get pushed up to the top of the fields. They needed to be removed before the farmer could plow. If you were raising livestock or sheep, the gathered stone would then be used to build the stone fences. In Chilmark, Aquinnah, West Tisbury, and Tisbury, where most of the stone was deposited by the glaciers, there are walls crisscrossing the landscape in every

Hammer blows drive the wedges deeper into the stone.
Hitting each wedge in the series a little at a time creates the
equal pressure throughout the stone necessary to split it evenly.

direction. I have seen farmers' walls on the Vineyard that range in height from three all the way to seven feet high. In general, three-to-four-foot-high walls are common. Those walls still remain standing on some of the oldest homesteads in the town of Chilmark. Covered with bramble and brush, they run every which way.

Traditionally, some of the larger stones have been shaped into smaller, more use-able forms by a very old stoneworking method called "feathers and wedges," in essence a technique that splits the stone in half or cuts different-sized thicknesses from one stone. Building foundations, farm gateposts, and, to some extent, walls all used stone that had been split by feathers and wedges.

A wedge is just that, a four-by-one-half-inch piece of metal that is very thin at its point and becomes thicker at the other end. The iron feather has exactly the opposite shape. It is thick at its bottom and thin at its top. To split a stone with this method I first have to drill holes in the stone as deep as the wedge is long. The wedges I use are four inches long. Using a carbide drill bit, I make holes about six inches apart along a line the length of the stone. If the stone to be split is four feet long, it would take eight sets of feathers and wedges to crack the stone apart. After cleaning out the stone dust, I insert a three-piece set consisting of one wedge and two feathers; the wedge sits between the feathers. All down the line, I put a set in each predrilled hole. After the sets are in place, I follow the series by striking each wedge with a stone maul, using one or two blows each, moving on to the next set in the sequence.

As the wedge is driven deeper into the stone, the feather's opposite shape allows the pressure that is being created to continue down to the wedge's tip and into the drilled hole until the pressure is great enough to finally break open the stone. The wedge alone without the feathers would just produce pressure at the surface of the stone and would not have the force required to split the rock. The stone's surface would just flake if only a wedge was used. Driving each wedge into the stone a little bit at a time will eventually cause enough tension to break the stone apart. The key to splitting the stone is applying consistently equal pressure to the sets of feathers and wedges in each hole.

When splitting a large stone into a newly created shape, you always anticipate that the end result will be what you hoped for. Most stone, like wood, has a grain that runs through it. If you can read the stone, recognize the pattern, and work with the grain, it will help you achieve the results you want from that particular stone. But sometimes, because of old cracks in the stone that you can't see, stones will break differently than expected. Many times I've gone through all the labor required to split a stone only to have it break in an unintended way. When this happens, all you can do is start over.

An old piece of granite whose face shows its history of being shaped by feathers and wedges.

"Most stone, like wood, has a grain that runs through it. Work with it and you're more likely to get the break you want."

From a design aspect, I like to combine the altered shapes of split stone with the totally natural shapes of other stones. There's a certain dynamic energy that comes through when they are used together, blending the differences into an overall pleasing shape or form.

It is always interesting and exciting to go to abandoned stone quarries, discover antique split stones, and then try to work them into projects. I still have special stones from fifteen years ago that I am waiting to work into just the right designs.

One last note on splitting stone with feathers and wedges. Before there were machines to drill the holes in the stone for the metal sets, all the drilling was done by hand. Using a chisel called a star bit and a stone maul, stoneworkers slowly chipped the four-inch hole down until it was deep enough for the metal set. In one old pasture off Middle Road by Fulling Mill Brook, there are numerous large boulders, some the size of cars, that have been split by feathers and wedges. Telltale signs of the drill marks remain on the remnant stones left in their grassy resting place. Whenever I see an old split stone, I appreciate the time, effort, and thought that went into the final shape that is seen.

LEFT: When the pressure is great enough, you not only feel the stone start to crack but hear it ripping apart. Instead of one stone, now you have two.

RIGHT: Splitting or cracking stones apart with a three-piece iron set is a very old stone working method. Drilling the holes and placing the sets is the first step of the process.

A HEARTH OF STONE

The Hollinshead Fireplace

A STONE FIREPLACE IS THE FOCAL POINT OF THE HOME. NO OTHER ARCHITECTURAL FEATURE MAKES AS DYNAMIC A VISUAL STATEMENT AS STONEWORK. THE IMPACT A STONE FIREPLACE HAS ON ITS SURROUNDINGS IS MORE IMPORTANT THAN WE IMAGINE. THE FIREPLACE SHOULD BE HARMONIOUS WITH THE OTHER COMPONENTS OF THE ROOM. THE DESIGN SCALE AND PROPORTION NEED TO BE IN BALANCE WITH THE ROOM'S SIZE, TEXTURE, AND OTHER CRITICAL FEATURES. IN CREATING A FIREPLACE YOU NEED TO FIRST BE COMFORTABLE WITH THE TYPE OF STONE, THE PATTERNS THAT THE STONES CREATE WHEN COMBINED, AND THE FIREPLACE'S PROJECTED OVERALL MASS. BLENDING THESE COMPONENTS INTO A DESIGN IS ALWAYS THE CHALLENGING PART.

A stone fireplace can appear heavy and bulky or clumsy and even feel oppressive if a design is not thought out fully. Good stonework has a sense of being solid and grounded, but it has a rhythmic, flowing lightness about it. When I describe stonework, I like to say the best pieces have a feminine quality about them. I want my fireplaces to fit in with the design of the home, not stand out brashly. A stone fireplace should be a visual starting point that complements and enhances the other decorative aspects in a room, and act as an anchor from which the other elements radiate. The design of the stonework should hold your attention and be fresh and interesting every time

Vineyard architect Linda Cohen remodeled this house situated
by a seaside pond, giving it a cozy cottage feel. I designed its
fireplace with colorful stones to convey the same warmth.

you enter the room. The actual stone-fitting style is critical in a fireplace because, unlike an exterior stone detail where there is generally some distance between you and the work being viewed, with a fireplace most people at some point have a close-up look at the fitting of the stone. The stonework in an interior space should be tightly controlled. A piece of work well done looks good from a distance as well as close up. Lots of times stonework seems great from a distance, but as you get closer the technique and fitting of the stones diminishes in their effect and quality.

Designing and crafting an individual fireplace starts with meeting and discussing the needs of a client. Soon after moving from Minnesota to Martha's Vineyard, I received a call from an island builder named Pat Mitchell. He had clients who wanted a stone fireplace for their new home. He asked if I would be interested in meeting them. I said yes.

The four of us met over a weekend. The clients, Marilyn and Warren Hollinshead, lived in Pittsburgh but spent many summers on the island, and had recently bought a piece of land on the Tisbury Great Pond where Pat would be building their new house. That morning we went to the building site and talked about designs, options, and choices of material. As with all of my potential clients, I took them to see some completed works. Pictures can't capture the way stonework feels in a room, and I want my clients to draw their own conclusions so I can get an idea as to what their tastes may be. This is always the starting point for me to work up a design for each project.

Towards the end of the day we stopped to get something to drink at Alley's General Store in the small town of West Tisbury. I was talking to Pat when I heard Marilyn and Warren say the word *Upsala*.

"You mean Upsala, Minnesota, population two hundred?" I asked.

"Why, yes," Marilyn exclaimed.

"That's where my mother was born," I said. "She grew up there, and I spent my childhood summers there at my grandparents' house and our cabin at Swan Lake. My grandfather, Tom Schiller, still lives near Upsala at a retirement home."

After the initial surprise, Marilyn told me that her great-grandfather's farm was just outside of Upsala, where he had homesteaded the property in the early 1880s. Marilyn's mother's family had been the Swedish immigrant homesteaders common to most of Minnesota, especially around Upsala. Her mother had moved off the farm after she got married; Marilyn's father had been the optometrist from a neighboring village. And it wasn't just the town we had in common. We discovered that Marilyn's maiden aunt, Ida Ryberg, had been my Grandmother Schiller's closest friend. Ida had lived on Main Street in a red house that reminded her of her beloved

Sweden. As we talked more about her family and our shared histories, we all marveled at what an improbable chance it was that both our families' pasts were rooted in the same small, remote hamlet in the hinterlands of Minnesota.

Over the next couple of days, I thought about the design for the Hollinshead fireplace. It would be a freestanding piece, which meant that it would have four visible sides. The fireplace would divide a large open space into a living room and a dining area, truly becoming, as all fireplaces do, the focal point of the house. The Hollinsheads wanted something simple with a country feeling that would blend with the home's rural farm setting. The room itself had a low cathedral ceiling. I feel that if a fireplace is a continuous unbroken line from floor to ceiling it has a tendency to look modern, which I felt would be inappropriate here. The mantel needed to cut the body of the fireplace into two parts, which would be a bottom and a top with the

RIGHT: Found treasures complement this fireplace's driftwood mantel.

OVERLEAF: Good design is about subtleties, things you might not notice the first time you look. This keystone is an example.

PAGE 85: The pre–Civil War chestnut wood, reclaimed from an old barn in Ohio, echos the fireplace's design of posts and beams. Integrating the wooden beams with the stone posts at the top helps to unify the materials. Woven driftwood caps the stone fireplace.

"Interior stonework should be tightly controlled;
fine work looks good close up as well as from a distance."

mantel as a horizontal divide. This would stay true to the spirit of the home. To enhance the old, country farmhouse feel, the materials needed to be weathered, aged fieldstone with a wooden-beam mantel. Then the idea hit me. Why not use some pieces of wood from Marilyn's abandoned family farm to make the mantel, something her great-grandfather had shaped with his own hands? I would need four pieces of wood, two at approximately six feet long and two at three feet long, between four and eight inches thick.

I called the Hollinsheads and told Marilyn my idea for the mantel. I already had plans to be in Minnesota with my two sons for the Christmas holiday, so I suggested she fly out and meet me in Upsala. She agreed, as she thought it would be very special to have something in her new house that directly tied into her family's past. However, Marilyn was not sure she would be able to find her family's homestead after all these years. This is where my grandfather enters the story.

I called Grandpa Tom and told him the whole amazing story and my plan for the mantel. He listened like the stoic Minnesota German he is, reacting as if I had just told him that it might rain tonight or that the Minnesota Twins won their baseball game against the Milwaukee Brewers in a meaningless contest with both teams fifteen games back in the pennant race in late August. (My grandfather never was much of a sports fan anyway.) "Ach, no really?" he said. To him it seemed like something as outrageously coincidental as this happened everyday. After all the time I've spent with Grandpa Tom, I should have known better than to think I would get some big reaction out of him. When I'd finished the story, there was a prolonged silence from his end of the line. Then he finally said, "She married the eye doctor and then moved." Of course he remembered the family. Most important, he agreed to guide us to the abandoned Ryberg Farm. I still smile when I think of how unflappable my mom's father was on the phone that evening.

In subzero weather and with twelve inches of snow on the ground, I loaded my father's 1981 yellow-and-tan Chrysler Newport with a chain saw, hammer, chisel, and other supplies that I might need for the trip and drove the five hours to Upsala from my family's hometown of Zumbrota in southern Minnesota. Everything was planned. I would pick Grandpa up on the way. Marilyn was coming from Pittsburgh, landing at the Minneapolis airport, renting a car, driving to Upsala, and meeting us at the only café in town. Surprisingly, it all ran like clockwork.

As the three of us left Upsala and headed into the country, it was like a scene out of the movie *Fargo*—the bleak, gray winter sky, the wind-driven snow blowing across the paved country road, and, of course, the cold. Before I knew it Grandpa was saying, "That's it, turn here." On the left side of the road stood the remains of

Marilyn Hollinshead's great-grandfather shaped this beam with an axe. The beam is now the mantel for their rounded-fieldstone fireplace.

Marilyn's family homestead. Through the drifting snow we could see an old dilapidated farmhouse, a barn, and a few other old buildings in various stages of implosion.

We turned up the driveway as far as we dared, stopping for fear of getting stuck in the snow. Grandpa stayed in the car; he wanted no part of the weather. Marilyn and I went to the house first. The windchill was brutal. In each building I poked around tentatively, not quite knowing what I was looking for, but knowing that when and if I saw it, my gut reaction would tell me it was right.

As we left the house, I was starting to get apprehensive. I wasn't finding the right pieces—was I leading all of us on a wild goose chase back to Upsala? To make matters worse, I was cold and it was getting dark. As has happened many times since then, something that I thought would be a relatively easy event was turning difficult.

I believe Marilyn had no idea about the doubts racing through my brain. Of course, I went on looking about as if it were all part of some master plan on which I was working. Using a bit of Grandpa Tom's midwestern stoicism myself, I showed Marilyn no panic, no nervousness or emotion, but just kept on looking for those accursed wood pieces. Grandpa, I am sure, sitting in the warm car with the motor running to keep from freezing, was wondering what was taking that boy so long, and

PAGE 88: This small dining room hearth took more than two months to complete. The fireplace's antique wooden frame separates the black slate stone from the white wooden walls.

OVERLEAF: The slate used for the majority of this fireplace came from a quarry in northern Maine. The small chips are leftover from the making of schoolroom blackboards.

RIGHT: Architect Bruce MacNelly designed this distinguished seaside home. Bruce and I collaborated on the design of the main living room's fireplace.

LEFT: Flowering forsythia sits in front of three separate varieties of freshly quarried granite.

*"Weathered, aged fieldstone and a wooden-beam mantel
enhanced the hearth's country farmhouse feel."*

LEFT: *The face of this fireplace is curved, so that no matter
which angle of the room you look from you look directly at
the stones.*

BELOW: *I walked the beach for more than three miles to find
this mantel, which has the same curve as that of the face of
the fireplace.*

asking himself why anyone would travel from the East Coast to Upsala, in the dead of winter no less, trying to find old, used wood. Why not go right to Cottle's lumberyard on Martha's Vineyard and get some new machine-milled oak or at least some pine beams. Now that would make sense. Trying to clear my head of these thoughts, I walked out of the third or fourth building that we had examined. There was only one more structure to explore. Looking at its snow-covered shell didn't help my sinking spirit.

It was a small, falling-down building made of round logs, which I could not use to make the mantel. A mantel needs to be relatively flat—on top so you can set things on it, but also on the bottom so the stones from the base of the fireplace can meet the mantel and nestle the wood into place.

With little enthusiasm, I stepped across the building's threshold and entered a semidarkened interior space lit now by a few rays of the waning winter sun filtering through numerous holes in a once-sturdy roof. After my eyes had adjusted to the dim light, they also widened in disbelief and then joy. The gut feeling was returning. Directly across from me was the building's interior wall made of, not rounded logs as I had expected, but hand-hewn timbers. Each blow of the ax had left a telltale mark on the face of the wood, like a signature left for the future to identify the one wielding the tool and to give meaning to one's life, as if to say, "I was here at this time and place. I did this"—a man's physical proof of his existence. Strangely, in some way, I felt a connection to that man at that moment. Maybe in all of our work, we were doing a similar act that will be captured in time, not to be critiqued as this or that, but to be judged as nothing more than work itself, done with some sense of pride and accomplishment—a sign for the future that we existed at this time, at this place, just like those before us and those to come after.

I had found the perfect pieces to make the fireplace mantel. After a few thankful moments, I realized that the most interesting and difficult part of the design was concluded. What was left was the physical part of cutting the logs from the ruined building, driving them back to my father's house in Zumbrota, crating the future mantels up in wooden boxes, and shipping them to the island.

Before this could happen, the logs needed to be trimmed to length and thickness. During the process, I discovered the wood to be an unfamiliar variety. I spoke to different area woodworkers who informed me that the building appeared to have been made from the little-known tree called the tamarack. Tamarack is one of the few species of evergreen-looking trees that loses its needles in the winter, only to have them reborn in the spring.

When designing for a cathedral ceiling, I like to break the surface of the fireplace into different sections. This one has four distinct areas.

ABOVE: Mini mantels ascend towards the top of the fireplace, each step holding a different carved bird.

LEFT: A series of stepped mantels breaks the plane of the face of this large fieldstone fireplace.

RIGHT: The stone panel behind the bench seat brings variety to the wood and draws the overall design together. My friend and master craftsman Tom Iammarino helped with the woodwork.

I called Grandpa that night to tell him my thoughts on what type of wood the logs turned out to be. Grandpa Tom replied, "I guess you didn't notice that the house was built in a tamarack bog."

Sure enough, when I thought back to the farmstead's setting, most of the trees surrounding the buildings appeared to be dead or dying spruce. The reality was that they were needle-less tamarack trees. In the warmth of my father's home, sitting in front of the blazing fire in the first stone fireplace I had ever built, I could not envision those towering trees on that bleak, cold winter day as anything but lifeless.

In some large way, meeting the Hollinsheads so soon after moving from Minnesota to the island, and sharing this experience with my grandfather and Marilyn in Upsala made the transition to my upcoming life on the Vineyard easier. The big question still remains, though: were the ax marks on the logs' flattened surfaces really from Marilyn's great-grandfather's ax? I want to believe that they are.

"A fireplace is the visual starting point to
the other decorative aspects of a room."

LEFT: The random small fieldstones are set back from the faces of certain vertical stones to create texture and shadows that add interest to the overall work.

RIGHT: Weathered, split granite and fieldstone, gathered and brought down from Maine, anchor the gable end of a handcrafted oak timberframe house.

ABOVE: *Small fieldstones packed between large granite posts create a backdrop for a bright cup of flowers.*

LEFT: *The massive pieces of old, weathered granite stones that make up this fireplace were lifted into place by a chain hoist attached to a steel I beam, which was removed upon completion. Some of the stones weighed more than one ton.*

RIGHT: *The exterior view of a fieldstone-and-granite fireplace which is part of an enclosed porch area beautifully designed by architect Ivan Bereznicki.*

ABOVE: *My client, an artist, and I worked together on this design. We chose to let the focus of the fireplace be the three stones that frame the firebox.*

RIGHT: *To get the rectilinear look from the fieldstone that is inside this fireplace's granite frame, I sorted through more than one hundred tons of stone, selecting each one for shape, size, and weathering.*

BELOW: Combining a wide range of stones and driftwood created an intense variety of patterns in this large fireplace that took five months to complete.

RIGHT: Three different stone types converge at the corner of this hearth's firebox.

"Good stonework has a sense of being solid and grounded,
 but also has a rhythmic, flowing lightness about it."

LEFT: *Architect Randy Correll, from the architectural firm of Robert A. M. Stern, designed this warm and interesting library. I chose the stone blend—Maine slate and Pennsylvania shale—to complement the rest of the room.*

RIGHT: *The color and tones of Pennsylvania shale are varied and rich. The stone came from an old fallen-down wall and stone windrow by the edge of a cornfield. Each stone was picked by hand, put on pallets, and shipped to the island.*

LEFT: *Antique split-granite posts create a frame for an inset of smaller native fieldstones collected from a grassy pasture field.*

BELOW: *Native fieldstone combines with an antique oak beam salvaged from a collapsed barn built in the 1800s.*

RIGHT: *This is one of the few fireplaces where I used a black mortar grout line. Freshly quarried granite makes up the body of work.*

LEFT: *Artist Richard Iammarino created the decorative painting around this small, cozy bedroom fireplace.*

BELOW: *A reclaimed gatepost from a farm in New Hampshire makes a mantel for a fieldstone fireplace.*

RIGHT: *By indenting accent stones in the lower two-thirds of the fireplace, I created a different texture than the flat surface of the top right-hand corner, adding a subtle distinction to the overall work of New York shale.*

LEFT: The raised black walnut panels and stone combine to make the fireplace the visual center of the room.

BELOW: The fireplace's arched opening, centered by its key-stone, makes an interesting reference point to the slightly asymmetrical, weathered-granite mantel.

STONE IN THE GARDEN

A Walled Garden Door

AFTER WORKING ALMOST A YEAR ON A VERY COMPLEX, TWELVE-FOOT-HIGH FREE-FORM WALL THAT CREATED AN INTERIOR GARDEN SPACE, THE DAY HAD FINALLY ARRIVED. TODAY I WAS TRYING TO BRING THE JOB TO ITS CONCLUSION. JUST ONE VERY IMPORTANT DETAIL REMAINED: SETTING THE FRONT ENTRANCE DOOR IN ITS PLACE.

The garden wall, built of both stone and wood, connects to a shingle-style house perched on a cliff with a dramatic view of the entire south shore. On a clear day you can see beyond Squibnocket Point all the way to the landmark Edgartown water tower. To the right, on the other side of Edgartown Harbor, is the island of Chappaquiddick.

Whit Hanschka, a metalworker, had just pulled into the driveway in his faded blue Dodge pickup. He was here to fit the massive wooden door with his custom-forged bronze hinges. The door itself was made from locust trees I had cut earlier from a forest lot up-island, near Aquinnah. They had been dead but still standing then, rendered lifeless eight years earlier by Hurricane Bob. Seeing the trees in the woods, oddly barren and denuded of leaves even though it was the middle of summer, I was reminded of randomly placed sculptures.

Locust wood is dense, and this door was heavy and tough to move. It would be helpful to be built like a linebacker for the New England Patriots, but unfortunately for me, my body is more like the five-foot-eight, 150-pound water boy. Countless times when I have been introduced to people as Lew French, stoneworker, their reply is something like, "Wow, I thought you'd be much bigger!" With a somewhat apologetic look on my face, I usually comment,

The main entrance to the garden. This is one of three openings that lead to the interior space.

ABOVE: A rich, deep-colored lobelia nestles next to a quarried drill-marked piece of curbstone granite.

RIGHT: The two ends of the stone wall connect to the house, making a completely enclosed gardening space, protecting the plants from the island's deer, rabbits, and sometimes intense winds.

"At certain times I wish I were!" The lifting work that I do requires physical strength. Whether it is true or not, I say to myself that if I were a little bulkier I could lift and set bigger stones.

The heavy door sat in the owner's garage, anchored in place by its weight. It seemed to be resting, waiting patiently for its chance to be hinged to the arched locust tree that would act as the doorjamb, supporting the denseness of the door, which weighed about two hundred pounds. The tree jambs had been set in two-and-a-half-foot-deep concrete footings many months ago. Today was the culmination of all this effort, and as Whit and I wrestled the door into place, I felt a certain smug sense of satisfaction.

From a design standpoint this had been one of my more difficult and challenging jobs. My task had been to combine all kinds of elements—large and small stones, locust trees, hand-split cedar shingles, cypress boards, and viburnum sticks—but still keep the design clean. I didn't want to fall into the trap of one of my client's favorite sayings: when you try to combine too many things, you just make mud. The setting of the door would be the crowning achievement of my work here, in effect signifying the end of my job. But of all my projects, this one had the most potential to go seriously wrong—to get muddy.

Whit is the classic stereotype of a blacksmith: six-foot-four, 210 pounds, big and strong. He possesses one glaring exception from the village-smitty image: he is smart. Soon enough Whit's intelligence would need to be utilized.

The door fit the opening relatively well; with a little grinding, filing, and planing, there would be no problem. I stood back and admired how it filled the space. The wooden door, now surrounded on all sides, was visually held in place by the patterns created by the massing of stones that defined this segment of wall as the center core

"The challenge was to combine many kinds of elements
and still keep the design clean."

of the overall design. The two materials, wood and stone, are very different in composition, one soft and one hard; yet they somehow combine to complement each other.

Almost like a circus showman, Whit started to slowly open the door, acting as if it was already hinged, so I could see its swinging motion. With pleasure I started to smile as the opening grew wider, revealing the beautiful lush gardens just outside of the enclosing wall. Then Whit stopped the movement of the door. I assumed it was all a part of the act. Time seemed to stand still. Almost as if waking from a pleasant dream, I could hear Whit's voice say over and over, "Lew, the top of the door is hitting the stone arch. I can't open it anymore." Ever so slowly the magnitude of the situation started to sink in. "What?" I said to no one in particular. "Oh my God! Why didn't I think of that? An arched door cannot be placed in the middle of a three-foot-wide stone-wall opening. Of course it can't open." The curving top edge of the door has to hit the stone above as it tries to swing open. Obviously, laws of geometry and physics had meant nothing to me until that point in my life.

I could see Whit's mouth moving but my ears couldn't hear him. My mind was reeling. Even I, in this numbed state, could see that the door would not even open wide enough to let my toy-sized dog Ruby, a Scottish terrier, push through.

This was bad. How would I explain to my client, while she is handing me a large check for the completion of the work, what went wrong? I could say, "Oh, by the way, it's part of my design for you not to be able to use the interior space." Perhaps as we are both standing on the outside trying to look in, I could just act dumb: "Oh, you

LEFT: The shuttered rectangle opening in the stone wall looks directly onto the ocean. The lush gardens enclosed by the walls were created by gardener Phyllis McMorrow.

BELOW, LEFT: A granite bench stone protrudes out of a garden wall and becomes the resting place for a gnarled stick of driftwood.

BELOW, RIGHT: Inside the walled garden, the verbena is in full bloom during the warm sunny island summer.

ABOVE: *The round window passes through the two-foot-thick garden wall to vistas of the interior garden space, locust arbor, and rectangular windows with views that lead to the ocean.*

RIGHT: *One of the interior corners has a waterfall splashing into a small pond with a surface area of approximately six feet by nine feet. The pond teems with fish, turtles, frogs and water plants.*

wanted an inside garden?" When she starts to ask about the door, I would just say, "No no no, this door was never meant to open. It's just a concept *alluding* to a door."

Now my mind really raced. It wasn't just these clients I had to consider. What about my potential clients? What should I tell them when it came time to show them other pieces of my work? Would I say, "Let's just look from the outside. Trust me, the interior is fantastic!" Mid-sentence I'd look at my watch and exclaim, "Good Lord! It's late! We had better get going to our next project," as I push them towards the car, dreading that at any moment they will ask, "How do you get into the garden? Where's the door?"

After what seemed like hours, slowly I began to hear Whit's steady voice, as though he were speaking from another room. Mentally I was lost somewhere, in a coma-like state. "Lew, I can fix it," Whit said over and over, almost chanting, until he finally broke the spell that I was under. Not at all perplexed by the door situation,

RIGHT: The arbor entrance, like all the posts used in the design, are made from locust trees. Locust is one of the most weather-resistant woods available. I especially like the tree's sculptural qualities.

BELOW: The stone pathway winding through the garden connects the openings to the outside. The garden's round window over the pond is in the background.

he continued, "If I move the hinge point nine inches off the door jamb, the door will fully open."

"What?" I asked.

He replied, "Help me put the door in my truck. I'll put the bronze hinges on in my shop, and the door will be done Thursday by noon." Of all the replies I should have offered, all I could come up with was, "Great! Thanks."

The door, now finished, did not need to be redefined as a piece of wall art or garden sculpture, but happily fulfills its main purpose of giving access to the enclosed space of the interior garden. On Martha's Vineyard, one of the gardener's most intense battles with nature is preventing rabbits and deer from eating cultivated plants. Luckily for my client, the deer have not figured out how to use the handle to open the door — not yet anyway. If they do, they will experience what Vineyarders

FAR LEFT: A detail of the stone from the privacy wall that is a screen for the outdoor shower.

LEFT: The huge bold granite slab makes a floor for the outdoor shower. After a day at the sandy beach, a shower is a must before entering the house.

BELOW: The vertical form of the tree separates and divides the horizontal lines created by the fieldstone and cedar shingles.

RIGHT: *The first view of the walled garden when approaching from the main driveway.*

BELOW: *Interior view of main door. Planting areas are built into some sections of the stone wall, with locust trees supporting the climbing vines.*

experience when we leave the island (where there are no large chain stores, only small shops more or less locally owned) and go shopping at a big store like Wal-Mart or Home Depot; a lot of us become overwhelmed by the size of the stores and the variety of choices they offer. If and when the day comes that deer gain access to the secured garden, just like their island human counterparts in a warehouse-like store, they, too, will be overwhelmed by the variety and lushness of the plant choices, not knowing what to eat first.

Set in the center of the thick stone wall, the door is now set back eighteen inches from each face. Many people comment that the door has a medieval or castle-like appearance. Friends and clients are always impressed at how balanced the pivots of the hinges are and how easily they allow the door to open. One of my friends calls the door a perfect exclamation point to the rest of the walled garden. To me, it is a reminder that no matter what mistakes we make in our lives, they are almost always fixable.

OPPOSITE: *The massive wooden door, which weighs about 200 pounds, was built through the collaborative efforts of island woodworker Pat Brown, Tom Iammarino, and me.*

ABOVE: *Metalworker Whit Hanschka made the custom bronze hinges off-center, making it possible for the arched door to open from its position in the middle of a three-foot-thick stone wall.*

LEFT: *A stone niche in the garden wall holds an antique iron urn that is used as a planter.*

"One friend calls the door a perfect exclamation point to the rest of the walled garden."

SETTING STONE FOR ALL SEASONS

A Pathway

TWO OF MY FAVORITE CLIENTS WANTED ME TO DESIGN AND BUILD A STONE SIDEWALK ON THEIR EXTENSIVE, UP-ISLAND, PASTORAL SEASIDE COMPOUND. THE PROPERTY, WHICH INCLUDES TWO HOUSES AND THREE OUTBUILDINGS OVER SIX ACRES OF LAND, ABUTTED ON THE OCEAN-FRONTAGE SIDE BY THE SHERIFF'S MEADOW SANCTUARY FOUNDATION. THE FOUNDATION IS ONE OF THE OPEN-LAND CONSERVATION GROUPS HELPING THE ISLAND PRESERVE ITS RURAL CHARACTER AND CHARM.

For this job, which would be the seventh major stone project and still not the last that I would do for them, the clients wanted a stone sidewalk to lead from the main house to the swimming pool and eventually to the guesthouse. The sidewalk was needed because of the morning dew on the grass. It is always hard to keep your feet dry. For me, this would be one more project with my clients in a continuing fruitful relationship. Like most of the people that I have been fortunate to work with, we talk, they express their thoughts, and then they trust me to do the rest.

As you walk from the door of the main house towards the future side-walk, you pass through a ceilinged breezeway for about twenty feet. Four years earlier, I had had the opportunity to design and construct a small rectangular-shaped courtyard enclosed by stone walls on the same property. The courtyard joins the house with a set of French doors that open into

Large quarried pieces of weathered granite were found in an abandoned quarry in Maine. When used with flat fieldstones, they combine to make a sidewalk with a gentle curve.

a large family room. Opposite the entrance to the main area is a massive stone fireplace that I also built. I coordinated both interior and exterior spaces with the unifying theme of the same stone, and I like to think of the two spaces as one. Included in the courtyard is a two-tiered water fountain that spills into a narrow stone channel and empties into a rectangular pool of water where goldfish, koi, and water lilies reside. In one corner of the courtyard, three stones form a group. The largest is the size of a kitchen stove laid on its side, and is built into the stone retaining wall to form a bench. The medium-sized stone is the size of a coffee table. It sits like an island in the sea of different varieties of low-growing thyme that replaces the standard lawn of grass. The third and smallest stone is a special find and gift to me from my friend Tom Iammarino. What makes the stone unique is the hole that goes halfway through its thickness and captures and retains rainwater. The naturally created hole was bored into the stone's softer shale by rapidly moving water and a pebble trapped in a depression in the larger stone. The pebble, moved by the flowing water, acted as a drill bit, slowly inching the hole downward. I have seen this feature in stones before, but I do not find it often.

My original plantings have really flourished. The Japanese fern, along with other varieties of fern, astilbe, thyme, sedum, moss, and shady perennials, has steadily filled the courtyard, making it seem older than it is.

Like the already-completed fountain courtyard, the design and materials for the projected sidewalk would be my choice. Making the sidewalk as flat and as permanent as possible would be the physical challenge. The sidewalk climbs from the house up a graded elevation to the top of a ridge, passing through an opening in an old, existing dry-stack boundary wall built by the early settlers as a part of a larger enclosure used for raising sheep.

"Set in a portland cement–based mortar on a concrete footing, this pathway should last seventy-five years or more."

In the beginning I did not have an overall concept of what the design should be, but I knew the path should not look like standard sidewalk made from stone. A concrete walkway has a general appearance of a rectangular ribbon cutting through the ground. In some earlier fireplace designs I had noticed through the stones' patterning that the interplay of the larger stones mixed with the smaller ones could possibly be used to make an interesting garden path or sidewalk. Now I saw my opportunity to use this concept. I wanted the design of this sidewalk to generate its own energy by creating a certain tension, achieved by using large, flat, strategically placed granite stones that interrupted the unbroken ribbon-like outside edges of the sidewalk.

All the stones for this pathway are set in a mortar bed on a concrete frost footing. You can tell where the large granite stone was split by the feather-and-wedge markings on its edge.

Now, as you stand on the main house landing stone and look over the walkway, your eyes are held for a moment by the large intersecting stones. They continue to follow the outside edge of the smaller stones. Combined with the energy produced by the curving shape of the sidewalk, this contrast draws the eye forward to its visual conclusion at the top of the ridge. By spacing the large stones, the sidewalk has the feel of being a path of stepping-stones, each large granite piece acting as a landing stone set in a sea of lush green grass, the counter being the small fieldstones highlighted against the blankness of the lawn and the larger scale of the quarried granite stones.

Unlike most stone walkways, this sidewalk was built on a concrete frost footing that extends into the ground two and a half feet. The stone itself is set in a portland cement–based mortar, on top of the substantial concrete footing. This technique for a stone sidewalk is the strongest, most permanent way to place stone in a landscape setting. Pressure created by frost rising out of the ground each spring causes cracks and movement in the stone, but under the right conditions, this pathway should last for seventy-five years or more. The large gray-and-pink granite pieces that form the vertebrae-like shape of the sidewalk vary in thickness from six to twenty inches, and each weighs up to three-quarters of a ton. The weight of the stone necessitated using a tractor backhoe to set the individual pieces in place. The smaller fieldstones were laid by hand. To finish the work, the joints between the stones were filled with

LEFT: When using old weathered fieldstone, I try to not shape or alter its visual face, but to fit the stone as is in a balanced, rhythmic way.

RIGHT: By enclosing the fountain garden space with shrubs and trees, the only view looking into this area is from the breezeway that connects the house to the stone sidewalk.

cement. The overall project lasted about two months, from choosing and collecting the stones to grouting the joints.

The job was completed just in time for the re-sodding of the lawn around the walk, cleaning up the property, and getting ready for my clients' oldest daughter's bat mitzvah, which was held outside. In the initial discussion about creating the sidewalk, the only condition that my clients had stipulated was that the stonework would be done for the spiritual and festive day. Lucky for me, it was.

While I was enjoying myself at the party that night, I could not help but notice the people walking on the sidewalk, wondering to myself if they realized that the stone walk was new, or if, as I hoped, they were thinking to themselves that it had always been there.

ABOVE: *The sound of water spilling from the fountain adds a soothing energy to the courtyard.*

LEFT: *One may glimpse a view of the fountain courtyard while passing through a second-floor hallway that leads to a home office.*

LEFT: *The patterns created by combining areas of small stones with larger fieldstones I find interesting and pleasing to the eye.*

RIGHT: *One of three interesting and beautiful accent stones featured in the garden space. The hole that you see in the stone is natural. Over the course of untold years it was created by moving water.*

BELOW: *The fountain's three vertical posts are framed by small fieldstones, which in turn are framed by large stones.*

AN INTERVIEW WITH LEW FRENCH

The Making of an Artist

DO YOU DESIGN AND BUILD YOUR PIECES YOURSELF?

Yes, almost all of the work in the book I designed and physically built. I generally work with one person who helps me. On a few different occasions, I have collaborated with certain architects and designers.

Designing the work is important to me, but being able to express myself through the physical work completes the process. Everybody working with stone has a different approach and technique, and that is reflected in the result. To just design a piece but not execute its construction never really felt right. To feel comfortable with a piece, I like to be involved from start to finish.

DID YOU LOVE JIGSAW PUZZLES AS A CHILD?

No, as a kid I did just enough jigsaw puzzles to feel frustrated. At some point I asked myself, "Why am I doing this?" and left them to go do something more fun. I liked to play sports, something more physical. One of the things I like about working with stone is physically touching it and setting it in place. At the end of a day of hard work, I like the feeling of being tired.

Small patterns of fieldstone fit into a frame of larger stones.

LEFT: *A hand-hewn mortised beam and a broken stone are combined to create a small sculpture.*

RIGHT: *I use a trowel to shovel concrete around and behind the stone to fill in any voids.*

ABOVE: *A hollowed-out stone with its profile chiseled into an oak driftwood log makes a tranquil reflection pool.*

LEFT: *I built this stone birdhouse for my son Truman when he was a small child.*

IS YOUR WORK INSPIRED BY STONEHENGE?

Whenever I am asked this question, I think of Asa, my older son. He was with me on one occasion when a person said my work looked like something from Stonehenge, and then asked if I had ever been there. I answered, "No," though I, like most people, have read some of its history and have seen some pictures.

Riding home in the truck together, Asa asked me about Stonehenge and what its meaning was. I told him that truthfully nobody knows for sure what it means. Much to my surprise, he continued asking me questions about what I do. I explained that when I do my work it is not about looking at pictures or other people's work and then re-creating what I see, but rather, trying to look inside myself and bring my own meanings and ideas to each project. How could I create something like Stonehenge when its meaning was lost to even those who had been present in its different stages of construction? We all put labels on things to make concepts easier to comprehend; although I can draw inspiration from what is left standing in place, its full meaning is only a speculation.

In the truck, I casually remarked to him that at certain times, even though I believe comparisons to Stonehenge are meant to be complimentary, they might also imply that I am trying to copy something that has already been done, a thought that is not so complimentary. Even though I believe there is really nothing new ever created, that we are just recycling ideas and concepts from our known and unknown past, there is still a uniqueness in a craftsman's own discoveries and added variations.

I was enjoying discussing my thoughts about stonework with my teenage son, but over the course of the next few days—a week at most—I realized it had probably been a mistake to discuss with him one of the minor issues I have with the Stonehenge comparison and if, at least in my mind, it implies that my work is some sort of copy. Quickly he made me understand that I had given him a new and potent piece of information to use to needle me. From that time until now, whenever he wants to kid me, no matter what the job is that I am working on, Asa will always comment, usually in front of other people, "Wow, Dad, that really looks like Stonehenge!"

An old stone well cover becomes an outdoor sculpture when set on two bases of weathered granite.

This question was asked daily by the carpenters and other workers passing through my work area for the past two and a half months; I had been working in a small bathroom space, roughly three-and-a-half feet by eight feet. From my standpoint, this had been one of my more interesting and fun projects. Located on the Edgartown harbor across from the lighthouse, the project in the basement of this stately old home unfolded just as the saying says: "Good things come in small packages."

The design was a mixture of the original house foundation wall that was made from island boulders. A new stone sink would be the central feature. Layers of stucco,

LEFT: *As you walk down the basement stairs, the view of the small stone sink appears through the glass of a reclaimed brass porthole from a boat.*

RIGHT: *The large, original foundation stone wall, driftwood, small stones and stucco are reflected on the mirrors of the bathroom door's surface.*

small stones, and driftwood fleshed out the design. In the span of the two-and-a-half months, I kept building up the layers of different materials to achieve the depth and dimension that I sought. Susan, my client, suggested adding a boat's brass porthole and mirrors on the interior side of the bathroom door to highlight the finished bathroom wall.

It takes a lot of individual stones to complete a piece. I try not to think of all the pieces involved or it can be overwhelming. You have to be in the right state of mind and get into the rhythm of laying the stone. When I have a project that focuses my energy, like this one, the hours in the day fly by.

However, it is true that there are some days I mentally just can't do the work. That's when I go home and do something else.

HOW DID YOU LEARN TO DO STONEWORK?

I am self-taught. I did not have any formal training or a teacher who I apprenticed with to learn how to work with stone. My father's friend Leonard Lundgren showed me the basics of masonry, and I developed my stoneworking style on my own. When I realized that I wanted to build things out of stone, I started to really pay attention to what I saw in my everyday life. I began to seek out information relating to stonework, mentally critiquing what I liked or disliked about the pieces I was viewing. I would look at magazines like *House Beautiful, Metropolitan Home,* and *Architectural Digest,* sometimes seeing things I liked but usually thinking there must be more interesting or exciting ways to display stonework. I knew from my early experiences with it that the power and energy of stone were not being used to its full potential.

I began to notice if the overall effect of a completed piece of stonework did not work in my mind, even if it had a really strong, well-thought-out design element to it. Sometimes it was because of poor workmanship, even though the technique used was interesting. Other times, it was the opposite: the stone-laying techniques were good but the overall design failed.

When I started to do stonework, my main objective was to be able to design and build pieces using the techniques I was developing so there would be consistency in the finished job. It made me wholly responsible for the end result. At this point, I have been focused on stones and how they affect my senses for so long that I have explored and experimented with a lot of different approaches and options relating to building with stone.

Two famous architects have helped me formulate my ideas about stone: Frank Lloyd Wright and Antoni Gaudi. They had two very different styles, careers, and lives, but both men influenced how I see and interpret stone.

What I see in Frank Lloyd Wright's work is a sense of the solid dominating presence of stone and how he chooses to use it. Wright mostly used limestone or sedimentary stones for their quality of horizontal lines. As an architect, he used stone to create focal points throughout his structures. Massive fireplaces and interior stone walls act as the center and heart of his homes. One example of extensive stone use is his home and workplace in Wisconsin, called Taliesin. He started the house in 1911 and continued to change and upgrade it throughout his long life.

One of the architect's greatest achievements was a stone exterior he created for a house in Pennsylvania called Fallingwater. It is generally recognized by architectural historians as the most important house built in America. Acclaimed to be the work of a genius because of his use of stones and other exterior materials to integrate the house into its natural surroundings, Wright's design incorporated an outcropping of stone from along the bank of a stream into the foundation of his design, letting parts of his buildings cantilever over the stream below. When I was in my early twenties, the pictures in a greatly detailed book dedicated to Fallingwater had a profound impact on my ideas about stonework and its relationship with its natural surroundings.

The architect Antoni Gaudi was a second major influence on my thinking about stone and the possibilities of its use. To me his work is very abstract and creative, mixing stone and other materials together to make forms and shapes that I find exciting

A stone hammer rests on a lichened fieldstone.

A painter's white drop cloth protects the wooden floors as the stones await their placements in a fireplace.

and pleasing. An architect willing to take risks in his building projects, he was a complicated and interesting man who had few, if any, peers.

I was shocked when I first saw Gaudi's work in a book about Barcelona, Spain. His unfinished cathedral, Temple Expiatori de la Sagrada Familia, is unlike any other church in the world. I was so impressed with the few pictures of his church that I went to the Vineyard Haven bookstore, Bunch of Grapes, and purchased a book about his work, simply called *Gaudi*. The book has more than 175 illustrations and pictures of his buildings. Seeing the photos of his structures, I began to understand for the first time what the words *organic* and *freeform* meant.

Gaudi's construction designs break out of the confined boundaries of architecture. His buildings have a fairy-tale or dreamlike quality to them. In some instances, they seem more like growing, living entities than man-made structures.

One other main influence on my work has been Richard Iammarino. Since moving to Martha's Vineyard over twenty years ago, I have been fortunate to have met and become friends with Dick, a talented and accomplished artist who works in a wide range of art media. It does not seem to matter whether he is using oils on canvas, carving wooden sculptures, or painting murals in some seaside homes, he is technically in command of his art materials. Dick brings his knowledge of the history of art and design into and out of his finished creations, making the new piece a totally original work that is built upon all that has come before us.

Dick and I have worked on many job sites together on the island, and he has done a wide variety of murals in numerous Vineyard homes. Some of his murals depict ocean scenes with seals, seabird, and fish, and one features a twelve-foot whale. There is a farmyard setting in a client's daughter's bedroom where her only request was that he paint the likeness of Ruby, my little dog, on her wall. Sometimes on certain jobs I have designed fireplaces around his painted work, and on other jobs he has painted his ideas around my stonework.

I am always impressed by his talent and knowledge of art. Being friends with Dick, spending time with him, and discussing art and the visual world have helped me a lot. Through our many discussions, he makes me think and see things in a different way, helping me analyze what I am doing with stone and letting me develop my ideas on a deeper, more complete level.

Though I am self-taught in stonemasonry, I have been guided by others in finding my voice. I find myself still learning. Every time I travel from the island, whether it is to California, Ireland, or Brazil, I find myself absorbed into these new natural-world environments. I try to stay open to what I see, feel, and experience. Utilizing what I see on my travels helps me in my stonework to emphasize the power and beauty of our physical world.

WHAT SUSTAINS YOUR MOTIVATION?

This question is usually asked when I'm doing extended projects, jobs that sometimes take years to complete. Lots of times I am hired to do only one facet of stonework on a project, but after its completion I get hired to do more.

When I use really small, fussy components like driftwood and pebble-sized stones, each fit of the material pieces has to be in the same range of standards. Whether it is a large stone or a small one I want them to merge to create an interesting pattern. It takes time to find and make the right fit. I assume that stonework looks frustrating to the person asking.

For me, though, the work that I do is generally challenging, not frustrating. The great thing about designing *and* building a piece is that I can, through the design, keep changing the final product to make it interesting to work on.

Once I am done with the project, there is a sense of completion. I like to look at and analyze what has taken place. I try to understand the strengths and weaknesses of what has been created. At the end of a project, I need to be my own worst critic. Most of my friends or clients are too nice and have only positive things to say about my work. To want to improve at anything, you must honestly evaluate your own work and learn from it. I have been very lucky to have good clients and good jobs throughout my career. This has enabled me to complete one interesting design after the other. At times, consistently having the freedom from the client to create different pieces seems like just a continuation of work, not a series of smaller projects. So in a bigger sense all of my work has just been one continuous job.

A low fieldstone wall encloses a single bench stone for viewing the ocean in the seaside garden.

At the angled intersections of the wall I made an opening to add interest to the design.

WHAT IS YOUR PREFERRED STONE-LAYING TECHNIQUE?

In my fireplaces and most of my other work, there is concrete, or "mud," as masons call the mixture of cement powder and sand. I try to have stone-on-stone contact on the exposed faces of the work, but to fill the voids created behind the stones I use concrete. When I stand back and look at my work, I want it to have the appearance of stone resting on stone, with no mud showing.

All of the work I do using mud as a backing for the stone starts with a concrete footing poured below the frost line. I never use concrete with stone unless it is on a frost-free footing. Using concrete to bind stone together without it being on a proper footing will eventually lead to cracking and movement of the stone. Using concrete makes the piece stable, safe, and permanent.

WHAT ARE THE PHYSICAL REQUIREMENTS OF YOUR ART?

I always laugh and understand why this question is asked. Most people are surprised when I tell them I see a chiropractor only once in a great while.

The question does make me wonder how many tons of stone I have handled, lifted, and moved. The thing with setting stone is that you usually pick it up, try the stone to see if it fits, set it down, pick up the next one, see if it fits, set it down—you get the point; you almost never move a stone only once.

As I get older, I have started to feel sore and stiff in the morning. I always try to stretch before I go to work. Flexibility, I believe, is the most important thing that I can try to maintain. I do stretch in the morning, but I need to learn more. At some point, it would be beneficial to do some stretching yoga. There are ways, though, to minimize the impact of so much lifting. When I am lifting a stone, I try to bend my knees, keeping my back as straight as possible, focusing my attention, and lifting with my legs. That, of course, is the goal but it is not always possible. At different times, I am forced to lift a stone from an awkward position. This was the case about ten years ago when I tried to roll a large wall stone end-over-end to place it in the base of a dry-stack wall. As I bent over and jerked the stone up, an audible pop came from my lower back. I knew this was bad.

This was the start of my seeing a chiropractor for about a year. I had ruptured one of my lower back ligaments from the strain of lifting the stone. During the next twelve months, my spine would pop out of place at different times because the ligaments were not strong enough to hold my backbone in place. It was a difficult time for me but, thankfully, I did get better. Basically, I see a chiropractor once in a great while. I am hoping it will stay that way.

Helping to guide a two-ton hearthstone, balanced and lifted by a chain attached to the backhoe, into place.

IS ALL YOUR WORK ON MARTHA'S VINEYARD?

Most of my work is on Martha's Vineyard, but in the past, there have been some interesting projects off-island that have been presented to me that I could not refuse. But the island is such a beautiful place to live and work that I always have mixed feelings when I leave for off-island jobs. However, when I actually start a job off-island, I find the new and different challenges stimulating. Working off-island at different periods in my life has helped me to refocus my energy and thoughts and to recharge my creativity, keeping me fresh. And being away from Martha's Vineyard and my family and friends makes me appreciate the welcoming lifestyle and rhythm of the island.

WHERE DO STONES COME FROM?

I get asked this question often, and it always confuses me. Is this person wondering what my son Truman wondered at the age of four when he asked me, "Dad, where do babies come from?" I mean, do I get embarrassed and answer, as I nearly did then, "Well son, when a mommy and a daddy . . ." stumbling and stammering, trying to answer a question that is maybe unanswerable? Back then, looking down at Tru, my diminutive son whose penetrating blue eyes stared back at me, I knew that even at his early age he would not be fooled by my elusive answers. He held my hand and shifted his feet, anxiously waiting an answer that would have meaning to him. I finally said, "Well son, it's one of those miracles from God."

But the person in front of me now is probably expecting something more along the lines of the big bang theory. I find myself saying, "Well, let's see. Billions of years ago the earth was formed. Tremendous heat was generated. Molten material, thus forming . . ." My mind starts to trail off, not unlike when I tried to answer Truman ten years earlier. I stumble and stammer with words of explanation until the person who is politely listening, I suspect, can take no more of my babbling and finally, but firmly, interrupts me to say, "No, I meant where do you get your stone from?" Instantly I feel the blood rush to my head; the same embarrassment that I felt years earlier in the presence of Truman, once again becomes apparent in my face.

Trying to save what little dignity I feel I have left, I end the conversation by saying in a muted voice, "Northern Maine."

One stone's shape accepts the second stone's profile in a seaside garden wall, visible beyond an old farmer's stone fence. Stone by stone, layer by layer, a wall of rhythmic pattern appears and stones that began as individual pieces can be seen as parts of a whole, the bigger picture. Here the stonework ends.

RESOURCES

The following listings are for people or businesses mentioned in this book.

BUNCH OF GRAPES
BOOKSTORE, INC.
44 Main Street
Vineyard Haven, MA 02568
(508) 693.2291
(800) 693.0221
www.bunchofgrapes.com
Independent bookstore

CAPTAIN FLANDERS INN
(508) 645.3123
www.captainflanders.com
The bed-and-breakfast's stone suite is the only place Lew French's work may be viewed by the public.

HANSCHKA
FINE METALWORK
Whit Hanschka
Holmes Hole Business Park
Vineyard Haven, MA 02568
(508) 616.6984
www.finemetalwork.com

IVAN BEREZNICKI
9 Wendell Street
Cambridge, MA 02138
(617) 354.5188
www.bereznicki.com

JOSEPH W. DICK,
ARCHITECTURE, INC.
17 Summer Street
Yarmouth Port, MA 02675
(508) 362.1309

MACNELLY COHEN
ARCHITECTS
P.O. Box 661
West Tisbury, MA 02575
(508) 693.4043
www.macnellycohen.com

PAT BROWN
P.O. Box 249
Tisbury, MA 02568
pnbrown@gis.net
Custom fine woodworking

PHYLLIS MCMORROW
P.O. Box 3104
West Tisbury, MA 02575
Landscape garden design

RICHARD IAMMARINO
P.O. Box 1122
Vineyard Haven, MA 02568
Custom murals

ROBERT A. M. STERN
ARCHITECTS
Randy Correl
460 West 34th Street
New York City, NY 10001
(212) 967.5100
www.ramsa.com
r.correll@ramsa.com

TOM IAMMARINO
P.O. Box 1122
Vineyard Haven, MA 02568
Master craftsman

TROW AND HOLDEN,
INC.
45 South Main Street
Barre, VT 05641
(802) 476.7025
Stoneworking tools, including feathers and wedges